READY, SET, DRAW!
ROBOTS AND MONSTERS

AILIN CHAMBERS

 Gareth Stevens
PUBLISHING

Please visit our website, **www.garethstevens.com**. For a free color catalog of all our high-quality books, call toll free 1-800-542-2595 or fax 1-877-542-2596.

Library of Congress Cataloging-in-Publication Data

Robots and Monsters / by Ailin Chambers.
p. cm. — (Ready, set, draw!)
Includes index.
ISBN 978-1-4824-0923-9 (pbk.)
ISBN 978-1-4824-0924-6 (6-pack)
ISBN 978-1-4824-0922-2 (library binding)
1. Robots in art — Juvenile literature. 2. Monsters in art — Juvenile literature. 3. Drawing — Technique — Juvenile literature. I. Chambers, Ailin. II. Title.
NC825.R56 C43 2015
743—d23

First Edition

Published in 2015 by
Gareth Stevens Publishing
111 East 14th Street, Suite 349
New York, NY 10003

Copyright © Arcturus Holdings Limited

Editors: Samantha Hilton, Kate Overy and Joe Harris
Illustrations: Dynamo Limited
Design concept: Keith Williams
Design: Dynamo Limited and Notion Design
Cover design: Ian Winton

Printed in the United States of America

CPSIA compliance information: Batch #CS15GS: For further information contact Gareth Stevens, New York, New York at 1-800-542-2595.

CONTENTS

8

MEGAMORPH

10

DRAGON

12

FUNNY ALIEN

14

RETRO ROBOT

16

FRANKENSTEIN'S MONSTER

18

AXEL R-8

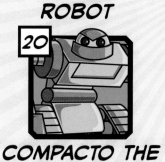

20

COMPACTO THE CRUSHERBOT

22

Q-T BOT

WEREWOLF

26

MEDIBOT

29

VAMPIRE GIRL

GRAB THESE!

Are you ready to create some amazing pictures? Wait a minute! Before you begin drawing, you will need a few important pieces of equipment.

PENCILS

You can use a variety of drawing tools, such as pens, chalks, pencils, and paints. But to begin use an ordinary pencil.

PAPER

Use a clean sheet of paper for your final drawings. Scrap paper is useful and cheap for your practice work.

ERASERS

Everyone makes mistakes! That's why every artist has a good eraser. When you erase a mistake, do it gently. Erasing too hard will ruin your drawing and possibly even rip it.

RULER

Always use a ruler to draw straight lines.

COMPASS

You can use a compass to draw a perfect circle, but it can be tricky at first. Try tracing a coin, bottle top, or any other small, round item you can find.

PENS

The drawings in this book have been finished with an ink line to make them sharper and cleaner. You can get the same effect by using a ballpoint or felt-tip pen.

PAINT

Adding color to your drawing brings it to life. You can use felt-tip pens, colored pencils, or water-based paints such as poster paints, which are easy to clean.

GETTING STARTED

In this book we use a simple two–color system to show you how to draw a picture. Just remember: New lines are blue lines!

STARTING WITH STEP 1

The first lines you will draw are very simple shapes. They will be shown in blue. You should draw them with a normal pencil.

ADDING MORE DETAIL

As you move on to the next step, the lines you have already drawn will be shown in black. The new lines for that step will appear in blue.

FINISHING YOUR PICTURE

When you reach the final stage, you will see the image in full color with a black ink line. Inking a picture means tracing the main lines with a black pen. After the ink dries, use your eraser to remove all the pencil lines before adding your color.

A texture is the way a surface looks and feels. It can be rough, smooth, shiny, dull, furry or scaly. Here are some simple tips to help you give your drawings texture:

OLD AND RUSTY

To make a robot look old and rusty, add dirty streaks of oil and patches of rust. Use green and brown pens or paint.

SHINY AND NEW

To make a robot shine, add white highlights to one side of every edge. Then, draw white patches with star shapes on them. Now your robot looks brand new!

HAIRY AND SCARY

To make a monster look furry, draw rough zigzags along the outline. Then, add more zigzags to the body.

SMOOTH AND SCALY

Add patches of small semicircles at different points all over the monster's body. This will make the monster look scaly all over.

MEGAMORPH

Megamorph has huge metal wings and mighty arms and legs. This giant robot is easy to draw, but use a ruler, as there are lots of straight lines.

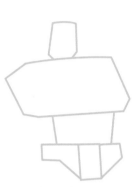

STEP 1

First, draw Megamorph's chest and lower body. Then, add his small, square head.

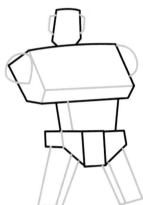

STEP 2

Now, carefully draw Megamorph's shoulders and upper legs. Add ears and chest details.

STEP 3

Next, add his big shoulder guards and neck. Draw his rounded knees and chunky lower legs.

STEP 4

Add his arms, feet, and fists. Don't forget the line that goes down the middle of his chest.

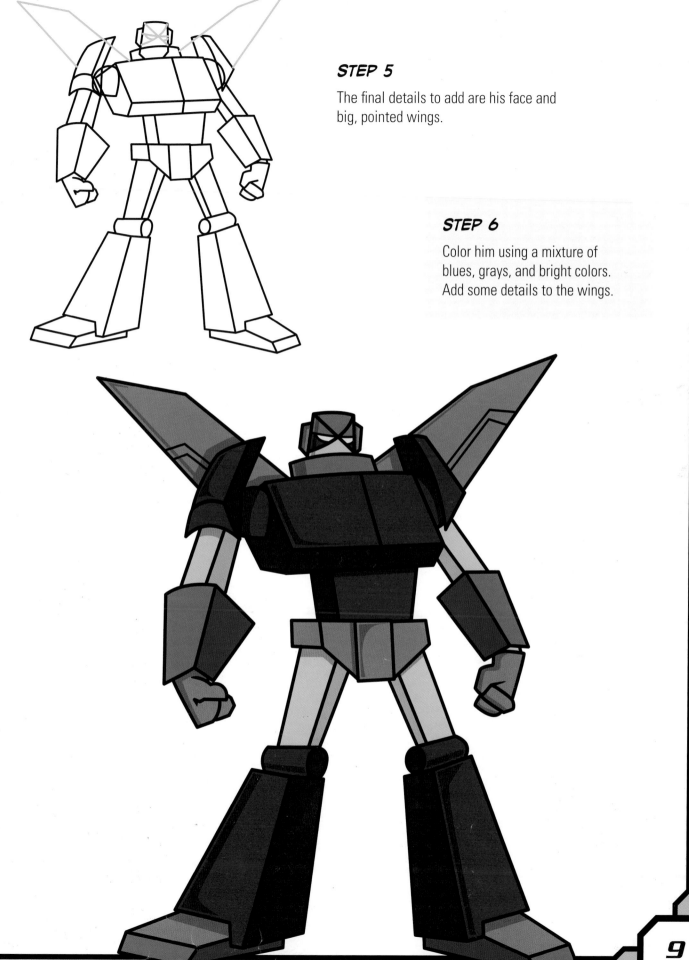

STEP 5

The final details to add are his face and big, pointed wings.

STEP 6

Color him using a mixture of blues, grays, and bright colors. Add some details to the wings.

DRAGON

Dragons are huge, fire-breathing monsters that look a lot like dinosaurs. They fly through the air, flapping their enormous, scaly wings.

STEP 1

First, draw the dragon's curvy body. Her tail should end in a sharp point.

STEP 2

Next, draw a circle for her head, shapes for her legs, and the top of one wing.

STEP 3

Add her long jaw, curves to her wing, and her lower legs. The two lines coming from her head are the beginning of her fiery breath.

STEP 4

Draw her lower jaw, clawed feet, and details to her wing. Add two circles and wavy lines for her fiery breath.

STEP 5

Bring your dragon to life by adding her sharp teeth, claws, and her second wing, and the details to her head. Don't forget the claw on her wing. Then, finish her breath.

SUPER TIP!

A dragon's wing looks a lot like an umbrella. Draw four lines joining at a point. Turn them into spikes. Add a claw and curved lines at the bottom.

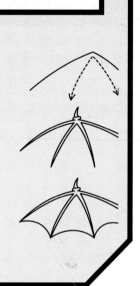

STEP 6

Add the triangular spines that run along the dragon's back. Then, finish her off in bold, bright colors.

FUNNY ALIEN

This is Blinky. He's an alien monster with seven crazy eyes. He has a big, friendly grin and thick, orange fur.

STEP 1

First, draw this shape to make the monster's body.

STEP 2

Add Blinky's wide head. Then draw his arms—one long and one curved.

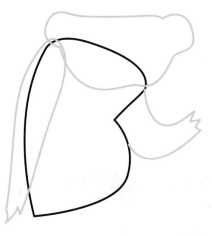

STEP 3

Now, add lots of circles for his eyes. Then, draw his legs, leaving a jagged line for his fur.

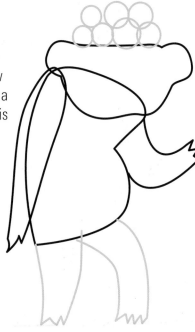

STEP 4

Add big, chunky hands and feet. Draw his claws. Then give him a tuft of hair on top of his head.

STEP 5

Dot his body with shaggy tufts of fur. Then, give him a wide, toothy grin. Draw black pupils on his eyes. Put them in different positions to make them look googly.

STEP 6

Finish your monster by coloring him in. The brighter, the better!

RETRO ROBOT

Retro Robot is a happy, shiny robot . He's always ready to lend a helping metal hand. Retro Robot has a wide toothy smile, bendy arms and large feet.

STEP 1

Start by copying these shapes for your robot's head and body.

STEP 2

Add small circles for his shoulders and hips. Then, draw his long, skinny legs.

STEP 3

Draw his big eyes and wide mouth. Then, add his long, bendy arms.

STEP 4

Give him an antenna, hands, and feet. Don't forget that toothy grin!

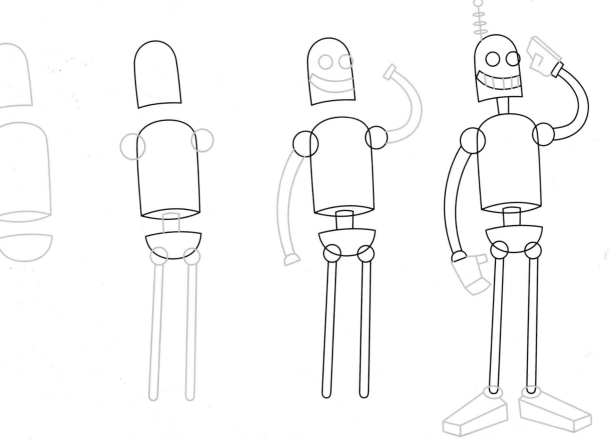

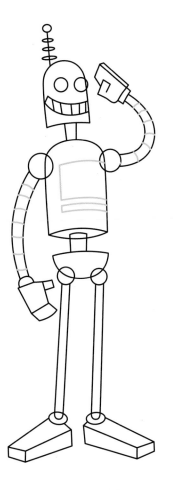

STEP 5

Add the final details to his arms and body.

STEP 6

Finally, add big black dots for his eyes, and color him.

SUPER TIP!

- Not all robots have faces like people. Here is a different head that will make your robot look more like a machine.

- You can add details to make little cameras and lights, too. He doesn't look so friendly now, does he?

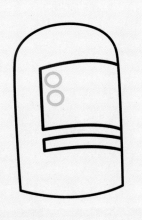

FRANKENSTEIN'S MONSTER

This monster is a crazy science experiment gone wrong! Dr. Frankenstein made this creature by joining bits of bodies together with metal bolts. Now it's your turn to make him!

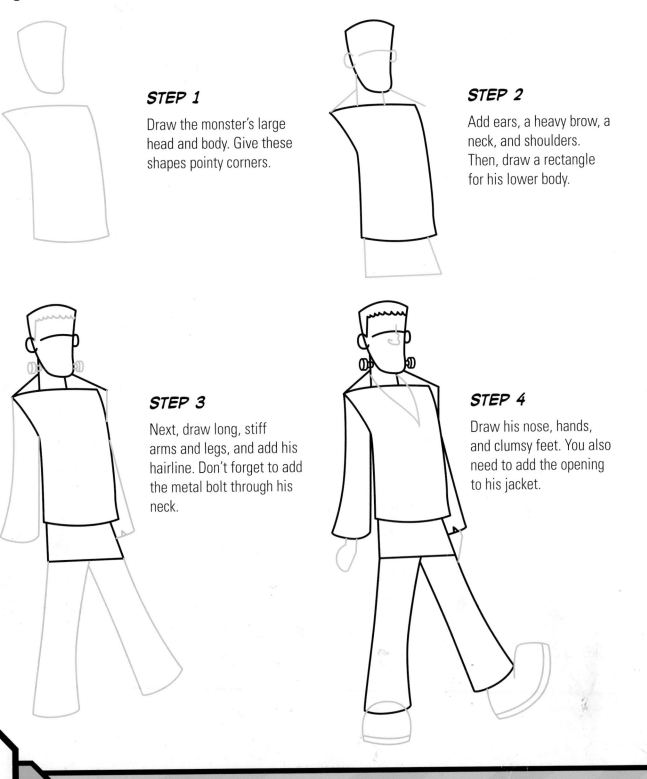

STEP 1

Draw the monster's large head and body. Give these shapes pointy corners.

STEP 2

Add ears, a heavy brow, a neck, and shoulders. Then, draw a rectangle for his lower body.

STEP 3

Next, draw long, stiff arms and legs, and add his hairline. Don't forget to add the metal bolt through his neck.

STEP 4

Draw his nose, hands, and clumsy feet. You also need to add the opening to his jacket.

STEP 5

Draw his fingers, and add the details to his face and clothes. Don't forget the big scar across his forehead.

STEP 6

Your monster is now ready to color. Use a gross green color for his skin!

17

AXEL R-8

Axel R-8 is a robot that was built for speed. With his rocket-powered jet pack on his back, he's always ready for blastoff!

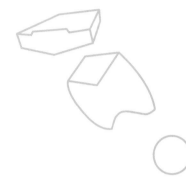

STEP 1

First, draw these shapes for your robot's head, chest, and lower body.

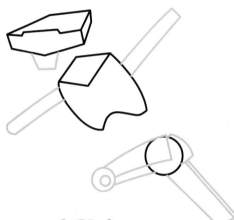

STEP 2

Draw long rectangles for his arms, and add his face. Then, draw his robotic legs.

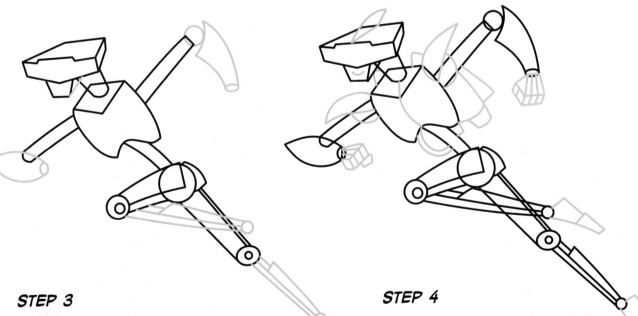

STEP 3

Carefully draw your robot's lower arms and lower legs.

STEP 4

Now, add hands and feet. Draw the jet pack, his mouth, the fin shapes on his shoulders and head, and some of the other small details.

STEP 5

Add the final details to his head, neck, and body.

STEP 6

Draw flames shooting out of his jet pack. Then color in your racing robot!

COMPACTO THE CRUSHERBOT

Compacto moves around on big, rolling caterpillar tracks. He has huge, crushing plates instead of hands. His mission? To crush anything that gets in his way!

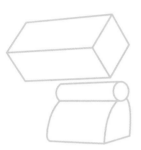

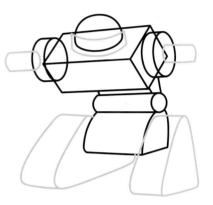

STEP 1

Begin by drawing a large block for his chest, a tube shape for his waist, and curved shape for his lower body.

STEP 2

Next, draw his head and round shoulders. Then, add lines to join the two parts of his body.

STEP 3

Draw a caterpillar track on either side of his body. Add upper arms and a band for his neck.

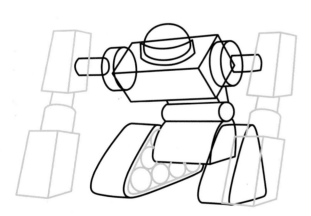

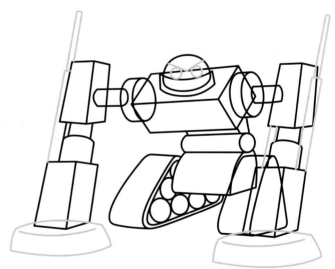

STEP 4

Add the circles to the caterpillar track. Then, draw his heavy arms.

STEP 5

Now, add the eyes and other details, including his crushing plates.

STEP 6

Add the final details to the tracks and other parts of the Crusherbot. He's now ready to color.

SUPER TIP!

Follow these instructions to make your robot look like he's really pounding the ground:

- Start with the basic crushing plate shape. Add some small lines to show the impact on the ground.

- If you want to show even more destruction, add some long cracks between the lines.

- You can even add some small puffs of smoke!

Q-T BOT

Q-T Bot is the perfect robot friend. His special antennae mean you can call him any time you need help. This cheerful robot may be small, but he's stronger than he looks!

STEP 1

Use a coin to draw a big circle for his head. Then, use a ruler to copy these shapes for his body and thighs.

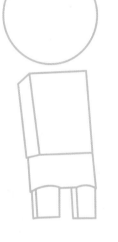

STEP 2

Take your time to draw his upper arms and lower legs. Don't forget to leave room for his big feet.

STEP 3

Now add his lower arms, feet, and big eyes. You also need to draw a line down the side of the leg on the right.

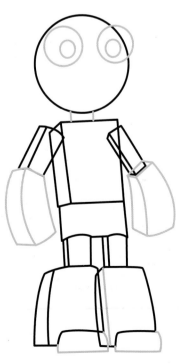

STEP 4

Give Q-T Bot a little mouth and helmet. Then, draw shoulders, arm joints, and a line for his waist.

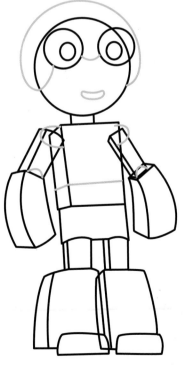

STEP 5

Add his chunky fingers, earphones, and antennae. Draw a line down the side of his pants.

STEP 6

Finally, draw a planet on his chest and color him. We used blue, but you could choose any color.

WEREWOLF

In horror stories, a werewolf is a creature that's part human, part wolf. He has a man's body and wolf-like features, such as a long, bushy tail and razor-sharp teeth.

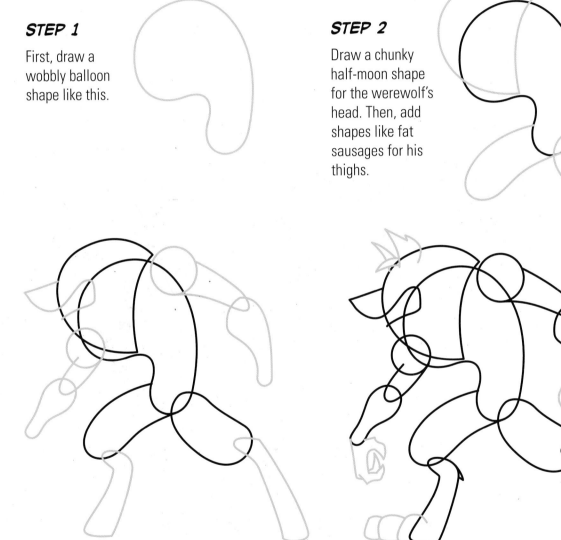

STEP 1

First, draw a wobbly balloon shape like this.

STEP 2

Draw a chunky half-moon shape for the werewolf's head. Then, add shapes like fat sausages for his thighs.

STEP 3

Draw his long muzzle and mouth, his shoulders and arms, and his lower legs.

STEP 4

Next, draw his hairy ears, hands, and big feet.

STEP 5

Now, add his long tail, eyes, and ragged pants. Then, add lots of tufts of fur.

STEP 6

When you color in your werewolf, remember to add lots of shading to make him really stand out.

MEDIBOT

Medibot is a caring robot that can hover on the spot. She has a smiling face and carries a useful medical tray. Medibot is handy for when you're feeling poorly!

STEP 1

First, draw a wide oval shape for her head. Now, add a longer shape for her body.

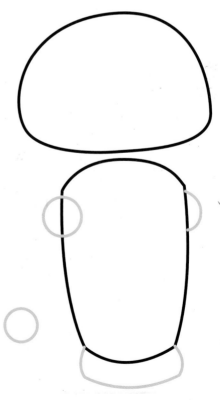

STEP 2

Add three little circles for her shoulders and elbows. Then, add a waistband.

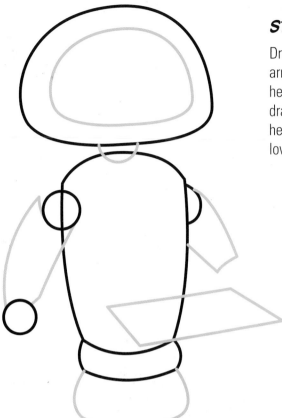

STEP 3

Draw your robot's upper arms and the outline of her face. Use a ruler to draw the tray. Then, add her neck and her lower waistband.

STEP 4

Add three simple shapes for Medibot's smiling face. Then, draw her lower arms.

STEP 5

Now, add the big medical cross on her chest and arm. Then, add her robot hands.

STEP 6

Trace the lines of her face in green instead of black. Then, add some color! Add lines beneath her to show that she's hovering.

With her well-cut suit and shiny, black hair, Vampire Girl looks chic and stylish. But stay away from those fangs because this girl bites!

STEP 1

Begin by drawing her slim body and head. Add a pointed ear.

STEP 2

Draw long legs followed by her thin arms.

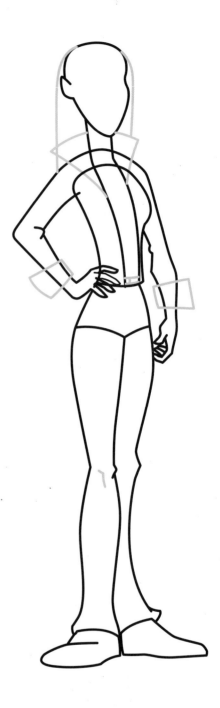

STEP 3

Join her head and body with a neck. Continue the lines of her neck to make the front opening of her jacket, and add her hands.

STEP 4

Give her a wide collar, large cuffs, and a belt buckle. Then, add her long, straight hair.

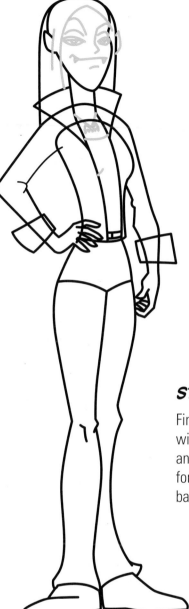

STEP 5

Finish your drawing
with her vampire face
and hairline. Don't
forget her fangs and
bat necklace.

STEP 6

Now, color Vampire Girl using
dark, creepy colors!

GLOSSARY

antenna An aerial that sends out or picks up signals.

brow Forehead.

cuff The end part of a sleeve, around the wrist.

fang A long, sharp tooth.

fiery Burning and hot.

hairline The shape of the edge of the hair around the head.

muzzle The nose and mouth of an animal, such as a horse or dog.

pupil The dark center part of the eye.

rusty Having to do with the brown, flaky material that occurs on some metal when it comes into contact with water.

spine A spike.

vampire In stories, a dead person who leaves the grave to bite and suck the blood of living people.

FURTHER READING

Ralph Masiello's Robot Drawing Book (Charlesbridge Publishing, 2011)

Spaceships, Aliens, and Robots You Can Draw by Nicole Brecke and Patricia M. Stockland (Millbrook Press, 2010)

WEBSITES

www.dragoart.com/robots-c401-1.htm

www.hellokids.com/t_1295/robot

www.sciencekids.co.nz/robots.html

INDEX